P9-CRQ-722

JOHN PIPER

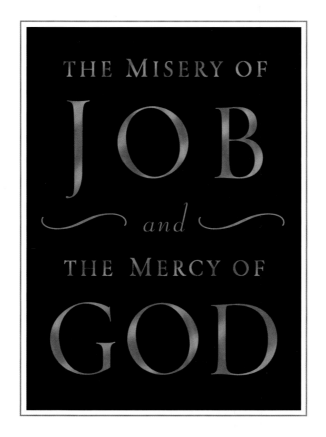

THE MISERY OF

JOB

and

THE MERCY OF

GOD

WITH PHOTOGRAPHS BY
RIC ERGENBRIGHT

CROSSWAY BOOKS
WHEATON, ILLINOIS

The Misery of Job and the Mercy of God

Text copyright © 2002 by Desiring God Foundation
Photographs © 2002 by Ric Ergenbright

Published by Crossway Books
        a publishing ministry of Good News Publishers
        1300 Crescent Street
        Wheaton, Illinois

Book design: Cindy Kiple

First printing, 2002

Printed in the United States of America

Scripture quotations are from *The Holy Bible, English Standard
Version,*® copyright © 2001 by Crossway Bibles, a publishing
ministry of Good News Publishers. Used by permission. All
rights reserved.

ISBN 13: 978-1-58134-455-4

LIBRARY OF CONGRESS CATALOGING-IN-PUBLICATION DATA

Piper, John, 1946-
   The misery of Job and the mercy of God / John Piper;
photography by Ric Ergenbright.
     p. cm.
   ISBN 13: 978-1-58134-399-1 (alk. paper)
   ISBN 10: 1-58134-399-X
   1. Job (Biblical figure)—Poetry. 2. Religious poetry, American. I. Title.
   PS3566.I59 M57   2002
   811'.54—dc21   2001008604

LB		17	16	15	14	13	12	11	10	09	08	07
16	15	14	13	12	11	10	9	8	7	6	5	4	3

This book is dedicated
to those who suffer loss and pain
along the path that leads to life.

He is not poor nor much enticed

Who loses everything but Christ.

It won't be long before the rod

Becomes the tender kiss of God.

CONTENTS

A WORD OF THANKS

The first time I saw and read Ric Ergenbright's

beautiful book, *The Art of God*, I knew I had

found a brother in spreading a passion for the

supremacy of God in all things. Thank you,

Ric, for embracing the vision unfolded in

The Misery of Job and the Mercy of God.

It is a great honor that you would beautify

these pages with your art, and God's.

A Word to the Reader

It is a great sadness when sufferers seek relief by sparing God his sovereignty over pain. The sadness is that this undercuts the very hope it aims to create. When all forty-two chapters of the book of Job are said and done, the inspired author leaves us with an unshakable and undoubted fact: God governs all things for his good purposes.

The text says Job's brothers and sisters "comforted him for all the evil that the Lord had brought upon him" (Job 42:11). This is the author speaking, not a misguided character in the drama. Whatever Satan's liberty in unleashing calamity upon us, God never drops the leash that binds his neck.

Jesus' brother James rounds out the picture with his interpretation: "You have heard of the steadfastness of Job, and you have seen the purpose of the Lord, how the Lord is compassionate and merciful" (James 5:11). In other words, the Lord is sovereign, and the Lord is sweet.

Pain and loss are bitter providences. Who has lived long in this world of woe without weeping, sometimes until the head throbs and there are no more tears to lubricate the convulsing of our amputated love? But O, the folly of trying to lighten the ship of suffering by throwing God's governance overboard. The very thing the tilting ship needs in the storm is the ballast of God's good sovereignty, not the unburdening of deep and precious truth. What makes the crush of calamity sufferable is not that God shares our shock, but that his bitter providences are laden with the bounty of love.

I have written for sufferers. I pray that you will be helped to endure till healing, or to die well. One who suffered more than most wrote: "To live is Christ and to die is gain" (Philippians 1:21). Which of these will be our portion, God himself will decide. "If the Lord wills, we will live and do this or that" (James 4:15).

The great purpose of life is not to stay alive, but to magnify–whether by life or by death–the One who created us and died for us and lives as Lord of all forever, Jesus Christ. I pray that his sovereign goodness will sustain you in the unyielding joy of hope through every flame of pain and flood of fear. To that end I set before you *The Misery of Job and the Mercy of God.*

As poetry, it is meant to be heard as well as read. To that end I have recorded my own reading of the poem on the accompanying CD. I pray that both the sound and the meaning will carry the truth to your mind and heart.

John Piper

PART ONE

O GOD,
HAVE MERCY
ON MY SEED

There was a man in the land of Uz

whose name was Job.

JOB 1:1a ESV

The sky above the land of Uz
Could change the way the ocean does
In moments, with a boding wind,
As though the blue of day had sinned,
And brought the blood of some great saint
Upon the darkening east – the taint
Of some Leviathan, up-swirled
Beneath the waters of the world,
Or worse, poured down like thick'ning gore
From some great struggle in the war
Of heav'n.

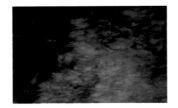

But Job had seen the years

Change dark and early-morning fears

To pleasant afternoons and clear

Night-skies, star-strewn and bright from here

To who knows where beyond the brink

Of earth and heav'n. So Job would drink

His desert-berry wine, and walk

Along his garden paths, and talk

Of all the years that God had made

His fields to bear the golden blade

For camels, oxen, asses, sheep –

Eleven thousand mouths to keep

With grain and grass and streams – and not

A flood or drought or wasting rot,

Or pestilence, or early freeze,

Or looting from his enemies.

And Job would lift his hands to God,

And wonder why he spared the rod

Of suffering. Each day he blessed

The gentleness of God, confessed

His hope in God alone, and said,

"O Lord, if this were lost instead,
And all I had was you, I would
Be rich, and have the greatest Good.
But I do love my seven sons,
And all my daughters, Lord, the ones
Above all land and name and wealth,
And even, God, above my health.
For them I praise and bless your name,
And pray that any sin or blame
In them would be forgiven by
The mercy you have shown in sky
And earth these forty years that they
Have lived now even to this day."

And every seven days Job made

A sacrifice for them. He laid

A lamb across the stone and prayed,

"O God, if they have sinned, and played

The fool and cursed your name, lay not

This folly to their charge, but blot

It out with this lamb's blood, and heed

My prayer: Far better one should bleed

For all, than all unpardoned live

And prosper without God. Forgive,

O Lord, and let your pardon pull

My sons from wealth and make them full

Of God." Thus Job would bow and seek

To save his children every week.

For seven days his sons would feast,

Down from the eldest to the least,

Each day a different son and spouse

Would play the host, and make their house

A banquet hall for all the rest.

The daughters too would come, all dressed

In finest fabrics from the looms

Across the land of Uz, with plumes

And jewels in their hair. And they

Would eat the finest foods and play

And dance and sing as if in all

The world there were no pain or gall

To see, much less to bear; nor was

Their father ever there, because

He carried in his soul a weight

Too heavy for the young, for late-

Night levity and bantering.

They knew about his offering

The lambs each week, and how he'd pray.

And so Job wasn't there the day

His children gathered to begin

Their seven days of feasting in

Their favorite place, when work was done,

The home of Zachan, oldest son.

That morning, early, Job had gone

Alone with sheep and knife, at dawn,

To make his sacrifice. And while

He prayed, God put his heart on trial:

"O man of God, today again

You seek the precious lives of ten

Young souls. Now tell me, with your heart,

Would you be willing, Job, to part

With all your children, if in my

Deep counsel I should judge that by

Such severing more good would be,

And you would know far more of me?"

Job trembled at the voice, and fell

Before the bleeding lamb. "Compel

Me not, O God, to make this choice,

Between the wisdom of your voice

And these ten treasures of my life.

Far better I should take this knife

And mingle lamb's blood with my own

Than put my children on this stone.

O God, have mercy on my seed.

I yield to what you have decreed."

The sky above the land of Uz

Had changed, the way the ocean does,

When some Leviathan, up-swirled

Beneath the waters of the world

Roils deep and turns the regal blue

To gray. And streams blood-red broke through

The dawn and flowed along the brink

Of earth and heaven as if the link

Were in dispute, and some great war

Were being fought to settle more

Than even blood-red skies would seem,

Or Job, awake, could ever dream.

That afternoon, beneath a gray
And boding sky – the time of day
When families begin to feast –
Job sat alone, and watched the east
Grow dark, and felt the outskirts of
A distant wind that made him love
His children more.

And then a man,
With torn and bloody garments ran
To Job and fell before his seat.
"O master, only these two feet,
Of all your servants still can run.
Sabeans struck, and everyone
Is dead, and all the oxen teams
And asses gone; I hear the screams.
O master, this has never been
Before. M'Lord, what is our sin?"

And while the question lingered in
The air, the silence broke again.
Another servant ran and fell
Before the man: "Job, whether hell
Or heav'n, I am not sure, but God
Has loosed a flame and awful rod
Against this house, and all your sheep,
And wool, and lambs, and all who keep
Them safe from wolves are burned to death
With fire, and I alone have breath.
O master, why? What have we done?"
And while he spoke, another one,
A servant from the camel herd,
Came running with his bloody word:
"Chaldeans took them all and slew
The servants. Only I got through
To tell you that we've lost it all.
O master, every bed and stall
Is empty now. What will we do?
What will we do?"

And as the hue

Turned crimson in the western sky,

Job waited wordless with his eye

Fixed on the dark and distant hill

Where Zachan lived, and ate his fill

Tonight with all that Job possessed.

And then the servant came, and pressed

His face against Job's knees and wept.

Job knew the man that Zachan kept

For special errands, so he laid

His hand on him: "Don't be afraid,

But speak." "Good master, I do fear

To speak what you might die to hear."

"Speak, man." And so the servant said,

"Your sons and daughters, Job, are dead.

A wind came from the wilderness.

We couldn't know. No one could guess

That it would blow like that. The whole

House fell at once, and every soul

Is dead."

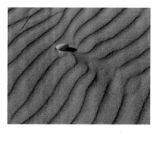

The servants waited now
To see what Job would do, and how
He might deal with his God. At last
He rose, and took a knife, and passed
It like a razor over all
His silver head, and tore his shawl
And robe, and fell facedown upon
The ground and lay there till the dawn.
The servants knelt by him in fright,
And heard him whisper through the night:
"I came with nothing from the womb,
I go with nothing to the tomb.
God gave me children freely, then
He took them to himself again.
At last I taste the bitter rod,
My wise and ever blessed God."

And now come, broken, to the cross,
Where Christ embraced all human loss,
And let us bow before the throne
Of God, who gives and takes his own,
And promises – whatever toll
He takes – to satisfy our soul.
Come, learn the lesson of the rod:
The treasure that we have in God.
He is not poor nor much enticed
Who loses everything but Christ.

PART TWO

THAT I SHOULD BEAR THIS PAIN, NOT YOU

The LORD gave,

and the LORD has taken away;

blessed be the name of the LORD.

JOB 1:21b ESV

The morning after Job had lost

His children and his wealth, he crossed

The half-plowed pasture to the east,

And made his way once more as priest

And father, to the altar on

The distant hill where he had gone

A hundred times at dawn to pray,

And sacrifice the lamb, and lay

His hands upon the head of that

Poor sheep, and by its blood combat

The sin of all his sons. From where

Job stood beside the altar there

At dawn this time, he saw across

The valley to the east the loss

Of all his earthly dreams – the home

Of Zachan, like a catacomb

Upheaved and strewn from some dark cave,

And broken like an open grave

Where all his buried children lay.

His hands hung limp beside the gray,
Blood-splattered stone. And then he knelt
And said, "O God, what you have dealt
Me in this murky day is not
What I had thought this bloody, blot-
Red stone would bring. Did I not pray
And sacrifice my lambs, and say
With sacred oath upon my life:
'Far better I should take this knife
And mingle lamb's blood with my own
Than put my children on this stone'?
But now what do I see below,
But servants climbing to and fro
Like ants on rubble foraging
For lifeless sons.

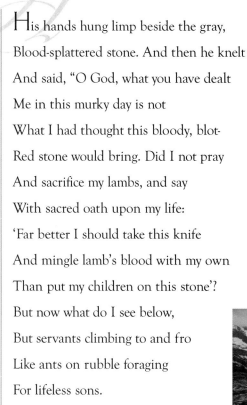

       O God, I cling
With feeble fingers to the ledge
Of your great grace, yet feel the wedge
Of this calamity struck hard
Between my chest and this deep-scarred

And granite precipice of love.
But I do fear the fingers of
My wife are not so strong, to hear
When she comes home, that every dear
And precious child she bore is dead.
Therefore, O God, once more, I shed
The blood of this lamb to atone
For her upon my killing stone.
I bow before you in the dust:
Have mercy to preserve her trust."

"They said that I would find you here.
What's wrong, Job? There's an eerie fear
On all their faces. Why are you
Here offering today? You do
This pri'r to Zachan's feast, I thought.
And that was yesterday. I brought
Him raisins from the river vines.
He told me they're the only kinds
He likes. And they won't grow down by
The . . ."

Dinah stopped and fixed her eye

Where Zachan's great estate had stood.

"O God . . . what in the name . . . Job, would

You please tell me what's going on!

What happened to the house? It's gone.

Where's Zachan, Job? And why were my

Three girls not waiting for me by

The gate when I came home today

The way they always do? Job, say

What you must say." Job said, "I fear

To speak what you might die to hear;

Or worse, might, hearing, live and curse.

O that I had time to rehearse

Some wise and gentle way to tell

You what we lost when that house fell."

Dawn broke, blood-red along the brink
Of earth and heav'n; and scarlet ink
Spilled upwards on the gray-blue shroud
Above the land of Uz. Job bowed
His head and gave way to great sobs.
He'd seen this sky before: "It robs,"
He thought, "like some celestial thief
Who thinks to gain by bringing grief,
And stealing what he cannot use,
Unless it bless him just to bruise.
God crush you, bloody messenger
Of pain! And, by my God, leave her
Alone. If one must suffer here
Still more, pluck on this flesh, and smear
My face with gall, and take my life,
But stay, and do not touch my wife."

These were his thoughts as they embraced,
Who knows how long. (There is no haste
In grief.) "Job." "Yes, Dinah?" "You know,
It was a long, long time ago
That you held me this way – so long
And tight, and without sex, and strong.
I might survive if you would stay
And hold me like this every day."

Job smiled and loosed his hold. But when
He tried to look at her again,
She gasped and pulled away. Job's face
Was full of sores, and every trace
Of healthy skin was reddening
Before her eyes. And then the sting
Began, and itching. Soon the pus
Was formed, and every sore was thus
A wormy fountain of a dread
And filthy oozing. Dinah fled,
And left Job standing in his plague
Alone. Within an hour one leg,

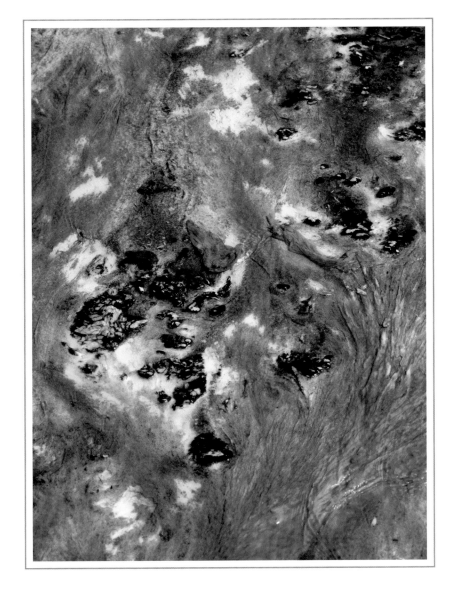

And then the other, flamed with the

Disease. The servants came to see,

And brought him food, but never got

Too close. He took the ashes hot

From off the altar where the sheep

Had burned, and rubbed them in, to keep

The itching down. And then he dashed

His pot, and with a shard he gashed

The biggest boils and let them bleed,

Like scarlet ink with earthen reed

To write his woes on parchment, gray

And ashen, like the sky.

That day
Was like a hundred years. At dusk
His wife returned. And she was brusque
And cool. "Do you still cling to God?"
She asked, and saw his wordless nod.
"I think you are a fool. How much
From him will you endure till such
A love as this from God, the Great,
Is seen to be a form of hate?
Here's my advice for you to try:
Curse God, tonight, and die. And I
Will follow soon – a widow robbed
Of everything." And Dinah sobbed.
And tears ran down Job's horrid face.
He pulled himself up from his place,
And by some power of grace, he stood
Beside his wife and said, "I would,
No doubt, in your place feel the same.
But, wife, I cannot curse the name
that never treated me unfair,
And just this day has answered prayer."
"What prayer? What did you bid him do?"
"That I should bear this pain, not you."

"O Dinah, do not speak like those
Who cannot see, because they close
Their eyes, and say there is no God,
Or fault him when he plies the rod.
It is no sin to say, my love,
That bliss and pain come from above.
And if we do not understand
Some dreadful stroke from his left hand,
Then we must wait and trust and see.
O Dinah, would you wait with me?"

"I'll try," she said, "I didn't mean
That you should die. I'm more unclean
Than you with all your sores." She knelt,
And found, between a boil and welt,
A place to put her kiss. "Is there
Some evidence that God could care
For such as me?"

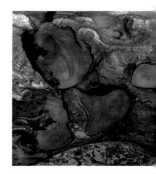

Job touched her hair:
"You are another answered prayer."

Sometimes the spark of faith is slight
And does not make the darkness bright.
But keep it lit and you will find:
Far better this than being blind.
One little flame when all is night,
Proves there is such a thing as Light.
Remember now the place and price
Where Jesus promised paradise.
One answered prayer when all is gone,
Will give you hope to wait for dawn.

PART THREE

O Spare Me Now, My Friends, Your Packages of God

Oh that you would keep silent,

and it would be your wisdom!

JOB 13:5 ESV

Some days the swelling pinched his eyes

Shut, so he couldn't see the flies

That gorged their smooth black bellies in

The putrid pus that seeped like thin

And yellow sap from crimson bark

Built up with dreadful days of dark

And drying blood. Only his wife

Dared touch his cloak, and with a knife

Relieve at times some throbbing boil,

And with her own bare hands pour oil

On his malignant neck and smooth

It down along his back to soothe

His pain.

As days and weeks went by,

The quiet news that Job might die

Spread down to Teman and the clan

Of Eliphaz the Wise, and ran

Its course along the western way

Among the Arab tribes, who say

Their father was the ancient chief

Named Shuah, known for proverbs, brief

And penetrating to the soul,

Where Bildad had his school, and stole

The hearts of all the Shuhite men.

The news went northward too, and when

It reached the town of Tadimor,

The old man Zophar wept, and wore

His grieving robe as he set out

To meet with Bildad on the route

From Babylon, and then connect

With Eliphaz – all three bedecked

For burying their friend, if they

Should come in time.

Eight weeks, one day,
And seven painful hours had passed
Since Job was struck. "How can I last,"
He often thought, "How can I take
One hour more and not forsake
My God?"

One afternoon Job raised
His pinched and swollen eyes, and praised
His God, because he saw three friends.
Job said, "O, how your coming lends
New strength to this old rotten corpse.
'Twas you, Bildad, who said, 'It warps
The mind to let it soak too long
In solitude.' Behold, no throng
Around the mighty Job, well bent,
As you would say, and had been spent
And broken too, in twain between
The loss and pain, but for my queen,
My servant queen, and mirror of
My God. But I do need and love
Your coming. Sit. And do not touch
This corpse. One, only, loves so much
As that."

Through seven days they sat,
And wept with Job, so broken that
They could not speak. Job felt the power
Of silent love, and every hour
Was like a gift.

But near the end
Of seven days a boding blend
Of gray and scarlet streaked the sky,
And Job waked with a trembling sigh:
"I've seen this sky before. It seeps
from some great battle in the deeps
Of angel-riven heav'n. And if
I know the signs, it means some cliff
Is in my way. O God, hold on
To me. I have no strength. This dawn
Is dark'ning over me, and I
Do fear another fall may lie
Before me in this path of pain."

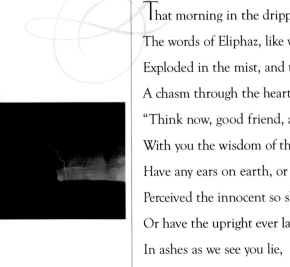

That morning in the dripping rain
The words of Eliphaz, like war,
Exploded in the mist, and tore
A chasm through the heart of Job:
"Think now, good friend, and let me probe
With you the wisdom of the wise:
Have any ears on earth, or eyes
Perceived the innocent so slain?
Or have the upright ever lain
In ashes as we see you lie,
Or suffered with such boils? Apply
What mind is left to you, and find
The cause of this great pain behind
Your seeming innocence. And seek
Your God in penitence, and keep
No longer secret all your sins."

Job didn't move, or speak. The winds
Of such incriminations crashed
Against his stagg'ring soul and smashed
The fingers barely grasping to
The goodness of his God.

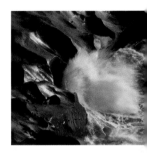

"That's true,
Great prince of Uz." The voice belonged
To Bildad. "O, whom have you wronged,
Once-noble Job? For I have learned
A hundred proverbs, all concerned
With why calamities befall
A man. And one thread runs through all:
The righteous have a prosperous lot,
But those who curse and sin do not.
The more your sin is large or small,
The more your comforts rise and fall.
Uncover what is hidden, friend,
And there will be a happy end."

With swollen eyes unblinking fixed
On Bildad's face, Job felt a mixed
Affection in his soul. "I've known
These men for decades now. This tone,
This thin and artificial slur
Against my life, does not concur
With years of empathy and love."
Job spied the bleeding sky above,
And pondered whence this turnabout
Had come.

And then Zophar spoke out:
"Remember, Job, the Lord is high
Above the earth, and he can spy
Iniquity in any place.
There is no hiding sin. The face
Of the Almighty is not veiled
By man, nor has he ever failed
To see and judge. Job, let your sin
Be put away, and hide not in
Your tents the bounty of deceit;
And then your days will all be sweet."

Job pulled himself up on one side
And trembling said, "How can you chide
A blameless soul, when God, for naught,
Has, like a wounded eagle, caught
It in his snare and plucked it bare
And broken both its wings? I dare
You, friends, to demonstrate your word;
Make known to me how I have erred.
I am not guilty as you say.
And should the great Almighty slay
Me in this cage, I will with my
Last breath protest your charge, deny
My guilt, and call your wisdom vain.
Clichés among the dullards! Plain
And bright as day – to all the blind.
Green words, unripened in the mind.
Whence comes this cure? A crystal ball?
Worthless physicians are you all."

Then Eliphaz set tenderness

Aside, and said, "God will not bless

A stubborn soul. How great must be

Your crime, to hide relentlessly

Behind the guise of innocent

Travail. I hear the bleak lament

Of widows that you must have mocked,

And orphans weeping that you locked

Outside your doors." Bildad joined in:

"Come, Job, what other cause but sin

Would make God crush your children there?"

He pointed to the valley where

The house of Zachan used to stand.

"You build your fragile hope on sand

If you cannot discern the hand

Of God in your demise."

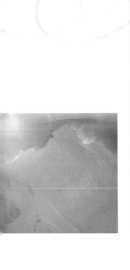

Job scanned

The faces of his friends, if there

Might be some opening, or prayer.

"O, I discern the hand of God,

My friends, I grant no other rod

The slightest countenance. What I

Deny is not that God on high

Makes winds to blow and lightning strike,

But that he rules as you might like.

I do not know why I lie here

And you sit there. But I am clear

It is not that I've sinned and you

Are clean. Your maxims, be they few

Or thousands, will not stand before

The bar of God. O that some door

Were opened to the court of God,

And I might make my case unflawed

Before the Judge of all the world,

And prove this storm has not been hurled

Against me or my children there

Because of hidden crimes. O spare

Me now, my friends, your packages

Of God, your simple adages:

'Be good and strong, but weak when wrong.'
They make good rote and clever song,
But do not hold the wisdom of
Our God. A whisper from above
Is all I have. Yet from it I
Have learned through horrid nights that my
Redeemer lives, and when my skin
Has been destroyed, then from within
Shall I behold him on my side,
And I will live though I have died."

O risen Christ, shine forth and be
A blazing warning by the sea –
A signal where the sailors cling
To life through reefs of suffering,
And need the blast of light and bell:
Beware, what here beneath may dwell.
Beware of subtle, shrewd assaults,
A half-truth can be wholly false.
Beware of wisdom made in schools,
And proverbs in the mouth of fools.
Beware of claims that rise too tall:
"The upright stand and wicked fall."
Beware the thought that all is vain;
In time God's wisdom will be plain.

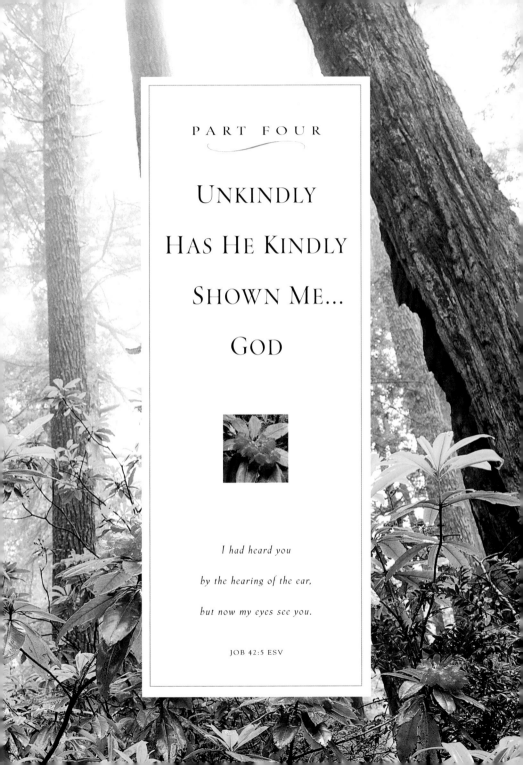

PART FOUR

UNKINDLY
HAS HE KINDLY
SHOWN ME...
GOD

I had heard you

by the hearing of the ear,

but now my eyes see you.

JOB 42:5 ESV

The deep blue sky above the land
Of Uz was cloudless. Stillness spanned
The circle of the earth with peace,
As if there had been made to cease
Some monumental strife unseen
Beyond the blue and arching screen
Of heav'n – a great inverted sea,
White-capped from some deep anarchy,
As though a wild Leviathan
Thrashed down its dirt to dim the sun
And bloody every morning sky,
But now a calm as far as eye
Could see, a silent azure pool
Of massive space above the cool
And restful evening, without pain,
Or any red and boding stain
Up-bleeding from the sutures of
The distant soil and sky above
The land of Uz.

Job felt the breeze

Against his healthy skin. "To seize

This moment would, I think, be here

An ample recompense. One year

Of misery, he thought, is not

Too long, to see of heaven what

I've seen, and watch the pow'r to heal,

And loving, feel what I now feel.

Unless perhaps six years have made

The recollected pain to fade,

And turn the memory of dread

Into a noble cause, and shred

The fabric of reality

And truth beyond identity."

He looked across the fields of wheat,

And endless rolling hills of sweet

Green pasturelands for all his herds

And flocks, and thought, "There are no words

To speak the substance of my soul

And joy to God, nor yet extol

His worth above the vast rebirth
Of all my dreams. No dancing mirth
Can suit or satisfy the kind
Of tearful pleasure that I find
When I recall what I have lost
By his decree, and what it cost
To see my God." He looked down at
The glowing little girl who sat
Before him on the grass – the first
Child born to Dinah since she nursed
The dead. Job wondered if there might
Be more in years to come despite
The treasure that Jemimah was.
He'd sometimes walk the hills of Uz
Alone, and lift his hands and break
Out singing that the Lord could make
A little girl like this from bone
And flesh that once could only groan
And grieve the loss of every child.

The little girl looked up and smiled:
"What are you thinking, Papa?" Job
Thought for a while, then said, "You probe
Perhaps, Jemimah, where the road
Is rougher and the mental load
Too heavy for your little mind."
"I like it, Papa, when you find
A story you can tell about
Your life. Why were you sick?" "I doubt
That you would understand," he said.
"Do you?" she asked. "Your little head
May not perhaps grasp all the Why,
But it may do us good to try.

"Your daddy, once, was very rich.
And you had three big sisters which
I loved with all my heart. They died
With seven brothers all inside
A great big house that fell because
A giant wind broke all the laws
We thought we knew. How little did

We know! And then one day amid
The grief I got so sick no one
Could tell that it was me. I'd done
All that I knew to do. But still
It came and vexed my soul until
I almost lost my faith."

"Do you
Think God made you so sick?" She drew
Her breath, and swallowed hard. "I know
You'd like to think that there's a foe
That hurts and God that heals. And that
Would not be wrong; but I have sat
And pondered months in pain to see
If that is true – if misery
Is Satan's work, and happiness
Is God's. Jemimah, we must bless
The Lord for all that's good and bad."

But, Papa, God's not mean or mad.
He's not our enemy. He's kind
And gentle, isn't he?"

"Your mind
Is right, Jemimah, but it's small.
He's gentle, kind, but that's not all.
I have some friends who thought they knew
The mind of God, and that their view
Of tenderness exhausted God's,
And that severity and rods
Could only be explained with blame,
To vindicate his holy name."

"So you think it was God who made
You sick?"

"I think God never laid
Aside the reins that lie against
The neck of Satan, nor unfenced
His pen to run at liberty,
But only by the Lord's decree."

"So you think God was kind to make
You sick," Jemimah asked, "and take
Away your health and all your sons
And friends, and daughters – all the ones
You loved?"

"Jemimah, what I think
Is this: The Lord has made me drink
The cup of his severity
That he might kindly show to me
What I would be when only he
Remains in my calamity.
Unkindly he has kindly shown
That he was not my hope alone."

"O, Papa, do you mean your friends
Were right?"

"No, no, my child, to cleanse
An upright heart of toxic stains
With searing irons is not like chains
Laid on the soul in penalty
For guile and crimes no one can see.
No, they were wrong. And kindly has
The Lord rebuked good Eliphaz,
And I have prayed for him, and all
Is well. You see, their minds were small,
And they could not see painful times
Apart from dark and hidden crimes.
Beware, Jemimah, God is kind,
In ways that will not fit your mind.
It's getting late, Jemimah, come,
I think I hear the bedtime drum.
My little theologian deep,
It's time to say good night and sleep."

"But, Papa, please, one more: would you
Tell me about the wind that blew –
About the whirlwind and the word
Of God. You told me once you heard
The very voice of God. What did
He say?"

"He said, 'There's giant squid

Beneath the sea you've never seen,

And mountain goats above the green

Tree line that bring forth kids on cliffs

So high and steep that little whiffs

Of wind would make a human fall.'

God asked me, 'Is the wild ox all

At your command? And will he stay

The night beside your crib and play

Or work with you on leashes made

Of hemp? And have the horses brayed

At your command, and do you make

Them leap like locusts? Do they break

Through shield and chariot because

You formed their neck? What ancient laws

Of flight have you designed for hawks?

Have you devised the way he walks

On wind and snatches up his prey

In flight? And could you ever play

With stars to loose Orion, seize

The distant chains of Pleiades?

"Where were you, Job, when I with mirth
The great foundations of the earth
Did lay, and all the sons of God
Rejoiced to watch a formless clod
Become the habitation of
My bride? Did you once brood above
The waters and appoint their bounds?
And have you joined the King who crowns
The mammoth sky with morning light?

"Come, Job, gird up your feeble might
And make your case against the Lord.
Do you know where the snow is stored
Or how I make the hail and rain,
Or how a buried seed bears grain,
How ravens find their food at night
And lilies clothe themselves with white?

"And finally, my servant, Job,
Can you draw down and then disrobe
Leviathan, the king of all

The sons of pride, and in his fall
Strip off his camouflage of strength,
And make him over all the length
Of earth and heav'n to serve the plan
Of humble righteousness? I can.
I make Leviathan my rod.
Beloved Job, behold your God!'"

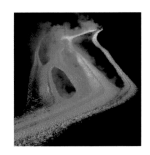

"And what did you say, Papa, when
The Lord was done?" "I said, 'Amen,'
And bowed as low as I could bow.
Come here, my lass, I'll show you how."

And when she crouched before his feet
He picked her up, and with a sweet
And tender grip he said, "Watch this."
And on her cheek he put a kiss.

Behold the mercy of our King,

Who takes from death its bitter sting,

And by his blood, and often ours,

Brings triumph out of hostile pow'rs,

And paints, with crimson, earth and soul

Until the bloody work is whole.

What we have lost God will restore –

That, and himself, forevermore,

When he is finished with his art:

The quiet worship of our heart.

When God creates a humble hush,

And makes Leviathan his brush,

It won't be long before the rod

Becomes the tender kiss of God.